Other titles in the UWAP Poetry series (established 2016)

Our Lady of the Fence Post by J. H. Crone

Border Security by Bruce Dawe

Melbourne Journal by Alan Loney

Star Struck by David McCooey

Dark Convicts by Judy Johnson

Rallying by Quinn Eades

Flute of Milk by Susan Fealy

Charlie Twirl by Alan Gould

Snake Like Charms by Amanda Joy

A Personal History of Vision

Luke Fischer

Luke Fischer is a Sydney-based poet and scholar. His publications include the poetry collection *Paths of Flight* (Black Pepper, 2013), the monograph *The Poet as Phenomenologist: Rilke and the New Poems* (Bloomsbury, 2015), the children's book *The Blue Forest* (Lindisfarne Books, 2015), and a co-edited volume of essays on Rilke's *Sonnets to Orpheus* and philosophy (Oxford University Press, forthcoming). His poems have appeared in leading journals and anthologies. He has been shortlisted and commended in a number of prizes and won the 2012 *Overland* Judith Wright Poetry Prize. He has been an invited speaker at literary festivals and conferences in Australia, Europe, and the USA, and has received research fellowships in Germany and an international writers' residency in Switzerland (Château de Lavigny, 2016). He holds a PhD in philosophy and is an honorary associate at the University of Sydney. For more information see his website: www.lukefischerauthor.com

Luke Fischer
A Personal History of Vision

Poetry

First published in 2017 by
UWA Publishing
Crawley, Western Australia 6009
www.uwap.uwa.edu.au

UWAP is an imprint of UWA Publishing
a division of The University of Western Australia

This book is copyright. Apart from any fair dealing
for the purpose of private study, research, criticism
or review, as permitted under the *Copyright Act 1968*,
no part may be reproduced by any process without
written permission.
Enquiries should be made to the publisher.

Copyright © Luke Fischer 2017
The moral right of the author has been asserted.

National Library of Australia
Cataloguing-in-Publication entry:
Fischer, Luke, author.
A personal history of vision / Luke Fischer.
ISBN: 9781742589381 (paperback)
Australian poetry—21st century.
Visual perception—Poetry.
Vision—Poetry.

Designed by Becky Chilcott, Chil3
Typeset in Lyon Text by Lasertype
Printed by Lightning Source

 uwapublishing

In memory of
John Blackwood (1940–2015),
teacher, geometer, friend

Acknowledgements

I would like to thank Judith Beveridge, Peter Boyle, Robert Gray, Ellen Hinsey, Adam Zagajewski, and Jakob Ziguras for valuable feedback on drafts of this book. Thank you also to David Brooks, Brook Emery, Dimitra Harvey, Simeon Kronenberg, and Tegan Jane Schetrumpf for feedback on individual poems, and to Jennifer Harrison for her support of my work. In June–July 2016 I received an international writers' residency at the Château de Lavigny, Switzerland, to work on completing the manuscript. I am grateful to the directors, selection committee, staff at the Château, and to my fellow writers in residence, for a fruitful month of writing and editing. Several poems have previously appeared, sometimes in a slightly different form, in journals and anthologies, as well as in a limited edition chapbook/artbook titled *Imprints*, which was designed and produced by Lutz Näfelt and Kerstin Göhlich and includes photographs by the Berlin-based artist Susanne Probst. I am grateful to them for their labours and interest as well as to the editors and publishers of the following publications: *Axon: Creative Explorations*, *The Best Australian Poems 2015*, *Connective Tissue: Newcastle Poetry Prize Anthology 2015*, *Contrappasso*, *Snorkel*, and *Southerly*. The book is dedicated to my late friend John Blackwood (1940–2015) and a number of poems, particularly in the second section, address and acknowledge the deaths of family members and friends. Finally, I would like to thank my wife Dalia Nassar for her helpful comments on the manuscript and her constant encouragement and support.

Contents

ONE
Retrospect
Head of Zeus 3
Translation 4
Horizon of Alps (K) 5
View from the Mountain 7
Annunciation 8
Madonna of the Goldfinch 9
Black Cockatoos 10
Heron 11
Five Glances 13
A Kind of Ritual 15
Sunday 17
Endowments 18
Rain and Memories 19
Certain Individuals 21
Cathedral Cove at Twilight 23
Madonna and Child 25

The same noise as chainsaws 26
Power Tower 27
After the Storm 28

TWO
Seed
Matthew and the Angel 33
Death 35
Wind 37
Night 38
Floating Seeds 39
Elegy for the Earth 41
Petrifaction 44
Deadwood 45
I 48
Waiting for the Train 49
Grief 50

Iris **51**
Fir **52**
The Field and Tonic **53**
The Shark **54**
In the Mouth of a Shark **55**
On Looking at a Photograph of Wisława Szymborska **57**
Confession of a Retired Scholar **58**
Mistranslation **60**
Sparrows **61**
Russian Beggar II **63**

THREE
Metamorphosis
Metamorphosis **69**
Respite **70**
Dawn **72**
Banksia Spikes **73**

On the beauty of eye wrinkles **75**
Glance **76**
Double Vision **77**
The Novice **79**
Scene in Music **81**
Labyrinth **82**
Anonymous **83**
Why I Write **84**
Turtles **87**
Breakdown **90**
In Wait **91**
Stones **92**
Val di Noto, Sicily **94**
Moon over the Sea **95**
View from the Shore **97**

Notes **99**

ONE

Retrospect

Head of Zeus

Turning to see
if you've missed anything
in a quiet room of the gallery,
you're startled by a marble head.
His locks are swirling cumulus; the curls
of his beard, entangled waves
whisked by winds. The dome of his skull,
the perfect ceiling above the clouds
from where he looks down at this tumult.
His wide cheeks hold the atmosphere.
Slightly unsealed, his lips are pregnant
with the pre-storm stillness, electrified air;
while his eyes sharpen on a toy ship
rocking unawares—in an instant
sundered.

Translation
Lavigny, Switzerland

In the morning haze
the Alps are smoky blue silhouettes
partly veiled by white chiffon swathes,
rising out of Lac Léman and of
slightly darker silk. Wrapped
in quiet they seem to be
emerging from sleep—
a lingering dreamscape
(the actors offstage).
Mont Blanc alone
in the habit of snow and ice
stands sober and vigilant
over the day. Though
their outline describes
a jagged seismograph,
with sharpened senses
I follow the grooves
like the needle of a phonograph,
attempting to translate
feeling's contours.

Horizon of Alps (*K*)
At the Château de Lavigny, Switzerland

Always at the boundary of vision, of thought
even when we look the other way. Though
often concealed in cloud and mist
veiled in haze, we know they endure.
Seemingly impenetrable matter
we sense a hidden truth, that they are minds
absorbed in contemplation.

On halcyon mornings Lac Léman
almost renders them as they are
in an image on diaphanous depth.
Their peaks shorn of vegetation, sheer faces
of stone, absolute architecture, prefigurations
of the crystals they hold.

Frozen tsunamis, primeval modernists
their abstraction rises above the lake and
its scattered sails—white chips in blue paint—
above the foothills' sprawl of villages, the tangle
of forests and human lives, above emotion.

Resembling a heterodox order of monks
great mathematicians, geometers whose bible
was Euclid, their enlightenment consisted
in continuous meditation on the axiom
of axioms, the formula of themselves.

With a sister order they communicate
in antiphon. Snow imparts: *Out of moisture
air and cold we make your structures light,
lighter than the empty bones of the tiny birds
that nest in your pockets.* They reply:
*We keep you from dissolving, lend
you a feeling of permanence.*

At times dark clouds envelop the summits,
tense as the disputes at the First Council of Nicaea.
On holidays the iconostasis opens
revealing Mont Blanc, the hooded high priest,
as censers spread their smoke
around the lower pinnacles.

Still epics, skeletons of mythic creatures, crystal skulls
pure forms, the moral law, metalogic, consonants
isolated from vowels. Your secret name:
the voiceless occlusive
k

View from the Mountain
Sicily

From here the sea
seems calm as the folds
in a renaissance rendering
of Mary's robes. And if you turn
to the west, the hills resemble
the turtles you saw huddled in the sun
at a pond in the Palermo gardens. The trees
are bonsai—intimate though distant,
their forms surveyable. The train tracks
and tunnels recall childhood afternoons.
You could almost bend down and
lift the valley chapel with your hands.
Its bells quietly toll. Counting six strokes,
you wonder if the quality of time
is dependent on the timekeeper.
The snaking cars are silent.
You only hear (despite the contrails)
the squealing of swifts and a breeze
through the bushes. When you sit on a stone
among wild flowers in mid-bloom,
the mosaic in Monreale comes to mind,
of God on the seventh day
seated at the centre of his garden,
how his surroundings seemed real
yet internal to his mind.

Annunciation
Fra Angelico

She does not gaze directly   at the gentle archangel
who appears in space   but is not in space
Her eyes are vague   as though absorbed
in reflection   yet not introspective
Her vision reaches   beyond the normal boundary
of the human mind   signified by the column
behind which   stands the angel
in the arched portico   open to air and light

Her dress is the pastel clay   of the convent
the colour of humility   (adopted later by Morandi)
with a hint of pink   affection
Her arms are loosely   crossed in reverence
Her midnight blue mantle   falls without resistance
She notices its weight   her posture
less than a person   feels a blanket in sleep

An empty vessel   all her mind is set
on stretching her gaze   beyond the normal boundary
Her eyes listen   to the other side of space
for a rustle   a call   a voice

And from the garden   in a rose dress and parrot-feathered wings
the archangel   has just flown in
He (or is it she?) bends   and with a slight smile looks
directly at her   confirms through his presence
Yes   *here I am*

Madonna of the Goldfinch
Raphael

The blue sky around her head,
a natural mandorla
framed by unmoving clouds.
Under a copper halo,
her hair's a fine bundle of wheat
in an afternoon glow. Her oval face
downturned eyes and tranquil lips
reveal an attentiveness as clear as air.
Her dress and mantle are a crimson rosella's
breast and wings. Is she human, or an angelic bird
landed in a Tuscan field? The horizon runs
behind her heart—exposed to the sky.
Her bare feet touch the soil. No longer reading
the open book, her right hand and eyes
keep a gentle watch on the baby
John the Baptist, who has brought a goldfinch
to her son. Standing upright, with one foot
on his mother's, he leans slightly into
the deep blue mantle washed over her legs
and while his right hand consecrates
the goldfinch, he looks at John,
no not at him, but past his appearance
into another space.

Black Cockatoos

A farmer told me once (I was twelve)
that black cockatoos were a sign of rain,
which made me wonder where they hid
on sunny days. I remember this
as I stroll a trail under a grey sky
that starts to spit, and surprise about
thirty of them congregated in a single tree,
clustered like large dark fruit. They seem
unrelated to their white raucous brothers
as they move discreetly and barely
make a sound—like an audience absorbed
in a song, a concentrated cumulus.

Heron
for Judith Beveridge

Standing still,
your figure is a cursive S
with a white lining
in art nouveau calligraphy.
Your tall legs,
the same lowercase l
as reeds along the riverbank;
their sharp leaves
templates of your face.

Your grey is not
the cool of our cities
but that of cloth
in a Cézanne still-life.
The homely shade
of chimney smoke.

The giraffe of wading birds,
you step deliberately through the shallows
then angle your head like a hunter's barbed spear
just above the streaming surface,
wait ... One quick jab,
the fish yours.

Had you chosen to be a plant
you'd be a Bird of Paradise
caught in a black and white lens.
Or a stalk in a bamboo forest.
As stone you'd be a crystal.

I recall the immensity
of your extended wings—
a slow-motion descending glide
above another stream, the air
seemingly viscous. And
how like a dancer—acutely
aware of her elevated status—
you sought a perch
in trees along the shore:
inspecting a few, wavering—
they were only fit
for smaller birds—
you settled on
an exposed dead branch.

Standing there, neck retracted,
you looked like a figure skater who has
just left the rink—shawled
with a jumper, absorbed
in the sense of a faultless
performance.

I look again along this river
and find you've dissolved
into the cloudy afternoon—
only reeds rippling
like grass snakes
in reflection.

Five Glances

The birch displays its leaves
like an elderly lady
holding up an heirloom
piece of lace.

***

A row of them
frozen in time
along a river—
waving their scarves
for a pageant.

***

They clap their hands
like small children
after a marvellous show
they didn't quite understand.

***

Always in rehearsal?
They wear laddered
tights with their white
leotards.

***

Today when I plucked
a catkin, it released
miniature doves and
cellophane butterflies.

A Kind of Ritual
Bondi Beach

This sundown gathering
of locals, travellers, recent émigrés
on the first balmy day—like the partly random
arrangement of stones on an ancient site
or a patchy memory of this place,
small groups seated in circles, recumbent in rows.

Brightly clad, semi-naked bodies
adapt themselves to the feel of sand; their curves
complementing the arc of beach, curl of waves.
Surfers paddle out on the gentle swell—wet skin,
shining amber. Catching slow breaks on longboards,
they ride with the ease of the hour. A woman
floating on her back savours the buoyant lassitude.

I think of Monet, Gauguin, Cézanne;
they would know what to make of this spot:
the lavender wash, bathers lifting their towels
the father with two girls ambling around the rockpools—
lingering over molluscs, anemones, cunjevoi,
a crab in a crevice with one claw
hanging out.

The buildings stacked on the headland
—neither elegant nor elemental—
but the sun gilds gutters and windows
like strips of gold ribbon and squares of gift paper.

Two skaters at the bowl
push one another, and a bull terrier
barks, tugging at his master's
lead. A Harley motors into
the carpark as the garish lights
of an outdoor bar stammer on:
A new scene—one for a van Gogh, perhaps.

Sunday

The beach is a slice of white bread
sprinkled with hundreds and thousands.
Sugar-brown bodies almost dissolve
in the swirling blue cocktail.

Waves toss paper lace over rock tables.
Children screech happy birthday,
swarm the playground. Ambling
the headland, tourists sample the views.

A goshawk is hovering high above—
wings trembling, eyes fixed
on a target. It will not miss
and no one will notice.

Endowments

The lorikeet's breast
is a sunrise over
the crooked horizon-line
of a branch. A photo
framed by green wings,
on a matching wall
of spring foliage. A holiday shot
by a Gold Coast tourist.
Its limping hop and speech
give away its origins,
its larrikin parrotness.

The formal magpie,
matching piano keys,
perches on its stage
in the avian Opera House
as the backdrop dims
to a watercolour violet
bleeding into blue. The strange
suppleness of its voice,
a burbling fountain.

Rain and Memories

Today I'll leave the world to the rain that recalls
long afternoons around a table and a half-eaten cake,
conversing with a friend ... We used to make sculptures

out of clay; under the press of finger and thumb
moist earth passed through a sequence of forms—
akin to clouds in a windy sky or phases of an embryo—

until it attained its fired shape. As a sign
for the studio door, we impressed wavy letters—
Gaudiesque—spelling *Timeless Realm*.

Earlier, in year 5 at school
a classmate discovering a mound on the oval
inaugurated a dam-building era:

numberless lunchtimes kneeling along a creek.
In hindsight we resemble figures in a lithograph
illustrating a chapter on the ancient Nile. Leafing

back through the book, I recall the various tribes,
my oaths and allegiances. There was also a battle:
we'd learned of the Norse gods—wise one-eyed Odin,

the thunder-god Thor, mischievous Loki, beautiful Freyja
(etymon of Friday) and their final conflict *Ragnarök*—
and one recess, as though a stormcloud had migrated

from the legend into our minds, we all turned
on each other, wrestled, threw stones—
girls and boys were injured, in tears.

Today I'll leave the world to the rain
and memories like plums in cooler climes
that ripen slowly over the summer and often fall

still green, to the ground ...

Certain Individuals

We rarely talk about what draws us
to certain individuals (and repels us from others).
We say: intelligence, positive outlook
trustworthiness, character ... But isn't it that
in one person we sense a clear glinting waterfall
refreshing to sit beside, in another something mysterious
as a fallow field at dusk? One's agility of mind keeps us on edge
like a squirrel poised on a bending branch, leaping the moment
before it would break. Another humbles us with thoughtful
pauses—a feeling of wisdom older than stone. One is curious
as a *Wunderkammer*—how did she learn eleven languages
when we have managed only two and a half? Another is a spring
always bubbling over into streams, tributaries,
a greater wonder than night to us—children of Saturn;
we're happy listening—attentiveness a glass
overflowing. One enters the room as dawn
breaks into a canyon. Another's bushy eyebrow
suggests an eagle's crown; his eye reminds us
of the meaning of *wild*—on arriving home
we find our Thoreau. One
never thinks an imprecise thought,
his words recall that alpinist who suddenly
reached into a crevice and presented us
with a cluster of crystals. Another seems layered
like soil preserving former times, rich and complex
as the books on her shelves. Of course
there are those who leave us indifferent
as a concrete wall in the mall carpark,
though they may be good people.
This is not an ethical treatise.

And those who inflame, disgust
but I don't recall them now.
What I'm trying to say
can't be pinned down (not in the sense
of *murdering to dissect*—those museums
of butterflies, though lifeless and cruel
are exquisite as illustrated manuscripts
antique brooches), is elusive as a scent.
Rose, jasmine, tea-tree, thyme
already too late.

Cathedral Cove at Twilight

Like an agnostic, reading
the mystics for the first time
you feel space turning inwards;

a touch of darkness
dyes the fabric of things
though there's still a way to go

before you reach the chapters
on the soul's night.
The headland watches

with the wind-hewn
features of an old recluse.
The wash and ebb of waves

loosens knots in the mind;
along with granules of sand,
draws hardened memories away.

The breeze runs its fingers
through your hair; the shore blushes.
You slowly detach like an unmoored raft ...

A long blond braid of water
unravels past a mossy ledge
and splits against a pool

that slithers on—scales catching the late light;
under the limpid body, sulphur
and sand are chequered like a fossil.

Gannets glide on silence;
their wingtips decipher
the braille of wind.

One with the threads
of their flight,
you plummet into the sea.

Madonna and Child
After Raphael

The sky is still and blue.
The wide valley—her open mind.
Streaming around her
crimson dress, the mantle
gathers in her lap and falls
unbroken to the ground.
Her hands hold the boy
(who will find himself)
with the gentle touch,
the non-attachment of water.

We leave the gallery.
The day is different.
We believe in peace,
freedom. As we sip
espressi, Spring light smiles
on the Renaissance square.

Back at the hotel
we switch on the screen:
a boy in Palestine
with stubs for arms
cries over his dead mother.

The same noise as chainsaws

A jet ski powers across the lake, tears
its fabric with doughnuts and tailspins,
gets airborne off its own wake
crash lands. Like timid children hiding
from their bellowing father, the voices
of lake and forest are silenced.
For a moment the rider stands still
as a flag on the water, surveys
his frontier, then thrusts back the throttle ...

Bobbing in our kayak, we look past
the racket to a sailboat in the distance,
its quiet traverse entrusted to the wind
that rounds out the right-angled triangle
like a shapely marble hip.
Hull and sail adapted to the elements
as the breasts and wings of the duck
family we can just make out
trailing by its side.

The jet skier blasts by again—
everything in reach of his self-
assertion. In the turbulence
we discern our troubled reflection.

Power Tower

A man of steel,
with its head and arms
it holds up thirteen power lines.
Anatomically basic:
spinal column, limbs, skull.
Made in our image.
Armless, it would be the shell
of a rocket, an industrial obelisk,
an infertile phallus. In this countryside
they outnumber church spires.
Modern six-armed gods
for whom we have no names,
they keep us from forgetting
who's in charge, our indebtedness
in our devices. Transmitting orders
more efficiently than commanders,
they surveil each other from hill to hill.
Perfect copies, bodybuilders posing for a mirror,
their iron fists suspend the weight of wires,
whose arcs, inverted rainbows, have harnessed
lightning. Up close, the clenched hands resemble
bulls' testicles—hunting trophies
won from Adad.

After the Storm

Sheltered, we glimpsed
a fringe of the storm—curtains of water
falling from gutters, metallic flashes
on a window of sky, gales
assaulting branches ...
Now walking the streets
we register the wreckage: broken batwings
of umbrellas weakly flapping on the ground
a pile of shards, scattered banksia pods—
undetonated grenades, flowering branches
of wattles and paperbarks
hanging on fences, bisecting paths
like severed limbs.

We find washed up along the disfigured beach
two sodden beams—ruins of a house?
a boat? a shed?—clinging to each other
with a bent nail, a piece of green fishing net
that's caught plastic containers,
a dead groper among fancy-dress wigs
of seaweed, a few bluebottles, further scraps
of plastic ... Behind the surf
float bubbly brown streaks
and a gull with cloud-grey wings
neatly furled. All this resembles
fragments of a trauma
mostly forgotten, not our own.

Sand covers the playground, promenade
and lawns. Like a scene
in an unfinished Bosch
an industrial beetle
rolls back and forth, pushing sand.
Another tractor builds
a model mountain range.
One digger stands still—
a gigantic wading bird
with its head bent down—
while a dragon spits a fountain of sand
and a frantic beetle
feeds its insatiable back.

Later we ride the train into the city;
the sky, though unthreatening,
is a canvas smudged with ash
and the skyscrapers are uniform
as prisoners in line. Tracks
the colour of autumn sycamores
recede. Abandoned carriages
with oxidised tearstreaks
collapse outside a station. Our
perceptions bleed into memories
of an Anselm Kiefer.

Perhaps only the partly-mad
homeless man on George Street
truly experienced the storm:
as the winds and rains
intensified, knifing his skin,
as snake-tongues of lightning
lashed from the skies and
a river flowed around his cardboard
raft, he could no longer distinguish
the weather from the screams and
blows of demons.

In the still air we sense
the aftertaste of wakefulness.

TWO

Seed

Matthew and the Angel
After Rembrandt

Some years ago
I thought I knew this image:

Not as background
on the evangelist—the source
of his gospel in the Word
through an intermediary.

Not as a portrait of the saint
with his totem.

But as a writer,
foremost a poet,
in the company
of his daemon.

See how lightly
the angel's right hand
rests on his shoulder.

See how her lips
silently whisper
in his ear.

See how he
is not permitted to turn
but angling his head
can almost glimpse her.

Or perhaps his listening
has become a kind of vision,
a mirror.

See his solemn smile
and how he holds his pen.
He has his *raison d'être*.

And notice his left hand
(pointing to the larynx)
at ease above his heart.

All this I felt I knew.

Now I write
to address the absence.

Death

My father had vanished.
Without warning.
At the age of four

I was shocked
into the truth
of life.

Others, old and young
seemed unaware.

They kept on living
as if there were no end.

Their smiles were false
like TV commercials.

Darkness
found a home
in me.

I saw the emptiness
behind glossy surfaces,
the vacuum seal
of irony.

I learned to love
the predawn hours.

In the darkness
I found my star.

In its soil
sprouts
a mustard seed.

Wind

Wind's the soul
that drives discarded things—
brittle leaves and rubbish across the ground,
a crumpled love letter, flapping sheets of news.

Wind awakens a palm tree
to its captivity, reminds the crown
of its destiny—limbs of a great insect,
the fronds struggle to break free.

Night

conceals branches in his folds
    cuts out turrets and places
the shadow puppets against the sky

He pours liquid darkness
        through the windows
submerges our house like a shipwreck

Only in daylight are ghost stories
unbelievable As things dissolve
you make out shifting faces figures

Your housemates sleep
   cocooned in silence
the hypnotist's captives

Sinkers hang from your eyelids
The membrane
between space and dreams

starts to tear and lead is mixed
into the conductor of thoughts They
fail to connect like someone who arrives

at a bus stop and forgets where he's going
Turned into a caterpillar
you crawl into a curled leaf

Floating Seeds

This is a poem for the dreams too large for people's lives
like the wings of a grounded swift, or a girl's feet
broken and bound in Lotus shoes.

This is a poem for those who felt
societal expectations were iron bars
but wanted the courage to escape,
pursue their calling.

This is a poem
for a wife, husband and daughter
dreaming of an ordinary life
while their neighbourhood is bombed
on 'humanitarian' grounds.

This is a poem for the paralysed orphaned boy,
even in his sleep
surrounded by upturned streets, bodies, rubble.

This is a poem for the abused
who cannot forget or heal.

This is a poem
opposed to surveillance,
the propaganda of terror
and programs to freeze
the wide river of dreams.

This is a poem for refugees
whose dreams are floating seeds
that find no ground.

This is a poem for those born in the wrong time.

This is a poem for a swamp wallaby
foraging near a wheatfield at dusk
that was eyed as a pest
and shot.

This is a poem
for the pines felled—
their needlework destroyed—
to build and record human dreams.

This is a poem for a friend
whose eyes and lungs are impaired
by the dust of regrets.

This is a poem
that offers nothing
but a castle in the air.

Elegy for the Earth

Geheimnisvoll am lichten Tag
Läßt sich Natur des Schleiers nicht berauben,
Und was sie deinem Geist nicht offenbaren mag,
Das zwingst du ihr nicht ab mit Hebeln und mit Schrauben.
—Goethe, *Faust*

The earth is a sleeping woman, let her sleep.
Let her tall hairs grow, let her green lungs breathe, let birds nest
   in her alveoli and praise the floral dresses she weaves and
   unweaves ... See that archipelago—a shoulder, hip, and heel
   protruding from the brine. Her breath fills the sails
   sends hulls over her shimmering sweat.
   When evening rises, air contracts and cools
   she breathes a sigh, rolls over
   in her sleep. In a valley nuns
   collect water from a crystalline vein,
   affirm to themselves their vows of silence.
The earth is a sleeping woman, cognizant in her sleep.
   She contemplates abstract Nordic light, raying
   through firs in a Finnish forest. She savours
   the spread of a Mediterranean lunch, spilling
   over into late afternoon and evening
   garnished with birdsong.
In winter she prints intaglios, etches
   snowflakes on plates of zinc. In summer
   she instructs Monet, paints large canvasses
   in watercolours. In autumn she works
   as a seamstress, mends clothes in a Romanian village.
   In spring she takes up the flute again.
Her dreams dissolve our contradictions.
   Each night all cows are truly black; by day every grassblade differs.
   She is leaf and flower, caterpillar and butterfly, stone and star
   an agitated squirrel, the rhythm of waves approaching a shore.

The morning light—her sharpened pencil—defines the geometry
   of the elements. At twilight she composes poems, mixes
   day and night, the finite and the infinite. At nightfall
   she dons her dark robe, plunges into the abyss beyond being
   and favours music that refers to nothing but the score of stars.
Each creature is a secret word, a cypher
   of unvoiced vowels and consonants. Our poems—
   partial translations—trace her turning tides, seasons, years.
Clouds stitch a duvet that keeps her warm
   draws her more deeply into reverie. Quartz crystals,
   her lucid dreams, advocate the Enlightenment
   exemplify structure, reason, clarity.
She has prototyped our inventions, modelled states.
   The plains of democracy, Brahmin
   Himalayas, hills balanced between
   earth and sky. Matriarchic beehives,
   ant-mound metropolises.
Becoming realities, her dreams
   transmute the coruscated surface of the sea
   into the scales of fish, dark ripples of an overcast day
   into a humpback's ventral pleats; raise fins into the air
   so they turn into wings of gannets and gulls—
   their flight the sentience of winds. While a goanna,
   moulded in lichen-covered stone, basks in warm rays
   the mammals embody its longing—the fire
   burning in the cave of their ribs.

The earth is a sleeping woman we won't let be.
    Those storm clouds are her troubled thoughts
    and nightmares. Submarines probe her lymph
    while surgeons dissect organs, test poisons, measure
    resilience by shattering bones, stitch her back together
    wrongly. Coughing, she lies on an operating table:
    her skin scarred, hair singed, missing limbs.

Petrifaction

After a Sculpture by the Sea, Bondi–Tamarama

With no one to turn to
she climbed the headland, sat down
at the sea's edge in the sharp winter winds
and clung to herself, knotted her limbs
around the sadness. Night passed.
Day returned. But wholly grief
aware of nothing else, she turned
into wood, and later, stone.

Deadwood

What is the obscure weight
embedded in my chest and the ball
and chain shackled to my ankle—
not nearly as heavy as those that hindered
prisoners, but creating a subtle drag
even when I walk with seeming confidence.
A limp that induces hesitation before
any affirmation of joy, that
slightly compromises every *yes*,
shadows it with a *no*. What
is this dull atmosphere—
like a room in need of airing—
incubating doubt? A voice
that whispers: *you should stop
writing, it's not worth the effort,
this won't work out.*

What has lodged this deadwood?
Has it ever been absent or consumed
in flames? Just the other day,
that trip across Lake Geneva
on a ferry from 1910, its pistons
heaving like rowers of stainless steel
in perfect time. No, not that,
but the views from the deck—
sunlit vistas of the Alps,
the white triangle of a yacht
under a shadowed mountain—
a Caspar David Friedrich
but alive and real. Climbing

out the windows of my eyes,
I met the prospects more
than halfway. The day
a holiday. The first time
I encountered that Schubert piece,
those passages like floating
down a wide river and hearing
the earth breathe. Writing
a poem in my youth, a communion
I felt, with a god or angel
who pressed its deep blue seed
into my mind ... What about
pain and grief, can they be entire?
Remember how overwhelming
sorrow married body and soul,
healed a rift in the universe.

But these scarce recollections
fail to convince. Normally
I keep a lookout for what could
hold promise. The anticipated
retrospective sparks interest,
is educative, but I'm not
wholly seized. After a meeting
with idealists and activists
I click on the news. Returning
to a verse that once set me
on fire I see only flames
that emit no heat.

How is it possible
in this infinitely varied world,
this multi-dimensional universe
to accrue deposits of apathy?
But arguments have little force.
The first principle that could tell us
why do something rather than nothing
is elusive or ineffective.

While this text
looks like a poem
it is a torch and my way
into the heart's subterrane,
a wavering illumination
of its resistant textures:
petrified wood and the marble
of ambivalence.

I

I is an upright figure,
a tall lean man
waiting for the bus
with his hands
in his pockets
to keep warm.

Or a solitary column
without a roof to bear.

My uncle 'the astrologer'
told me as a child
the 'I' was the true self,
a star that when i grew up
would alight on my head.

Later I saw
Blake's engraved frontispiece
for the *Songs of Experience*
and thought he must be right.

But these days
it seems
a charred post
in a vast waste,
a forsaken sign.

Waiting for the Train

In his mind
his body's already mangled;
his dreams are diary entries
torn and scattered on the city
streets; his heart's a broken
clock, ticking too fast, ringing
at ungodly hours; his life—
a web of subplots
spun by the black spiders
of addiction; a fly
at the centre, he
breaks free.

Grief

After thirty-six years
I've learned to accept
the gift of grief

The heart's fall
like a coconut
breaking
on the ground

The dark pool
one finds
on a late summer night
and swims—

pool without shadows
or boundaries

One feeling—
bodily, immaterial
whole

Iris

Concentrate of this evening's sky
risen from the soil. Purple
strange to our earthly affairs.
My eye finds rest
in your elaborate bed,
enfolded in deathly peace.

Fir

Your branches
like tiered roofs
of a Chinese temple,
cupped beneath the sky
and sleeved with snow.

An El Greco figure
beside the oaks and birches,
your single mission's
apparent each night:
the ascent of earth to star.

Through the blizzards
ever green, your ascetic fingers
never part from prayer.

```
        played vibrato by its wings ...    THEN
           the suspense of a seventh             glissandos
             and fluttering hovers—                      away
       a hawk glides up                              unresolved
Like a rising swing
```

The Field and Tonic

The Shark

(Earlier I'd found
a washed-up
egg case, that sculpted
whirlpool—vortex
glossy and still.)
A dark patch of seaweed
vague silhouette
but it moves
as cloud-shadow
in waist-deep water
its dorsal fin
invisible.
Along the shore
we follow it:
menacing and sublime
one with its sea.

In the Mouth of a Shark

I sit in the mouth of a great white shark,
a jaw of sandstone between Bondi and Tamarama,
before me the spread blue silk of the sea
here and there gashed by teeth, and to the south
Waverley Cemetery. Why do sun-illumined
tombstones emanate such tranquillity?
Not only here where they extinguish
the moth-like frenzy around prime real estate
but also in Paris, Philadelphia, Rome?
What alchemy
occurs in the mingling
of sun, earth and bones?

The body of a school friend
is buried there, who, on first impression
could've been mistaken for a typical Aussie bloke,
but his gregarious nature, his wide bright soul
would expand the dimensions of a room. A rare
heart virus intruded his twenties and he
suddenly died in his thirty-fourth year. I recall
our conversations about death—even before
he was ill—whether dreams of the dead
might be signs of contact, an afterlife.
After he died we spoke in dreams
or my dream-self spoke to images of him
at parties reminiscent of our youth.

When another friend died—
at eighty-seven,
a scientist not an artist—
I dreamed he held a solo exhibition
and personally showed me
a few of the pictures
relating moments in his life,
then through the bustling gallery
I walked alone from room to room.

A close friend and geometer,
the most youthful person I knew,
in months of the diagnosis
died of cancer at seventy-four.
Weeks passed devoid of dreams,
then one night in my lucid sleep
he cloaked himself in his former image.

Beneath the sun's glaring eye
the sea now shimmers like scales,
its blue glass is blown into brief prototypes—
the fin of a whale, a dolphin's back—
turned and shattered on the rocks below.

A cormorant drifts, dives and comes up
elsewhere.

On Looking at a Photograph of Wisława Szymborska

It's strange that poets
used to have their portraits done
with a cigarette in hand—
advertising the addiction,
suggesting inspiration at the strike
of a match, vaporous smoke
as a factor in winning a prize.
They knew it was unhealthy
and we know the deeper reason:
a demonstration of willingness
to embrace mortality—avowal
of the bond between poetry and death.
Still, it's surprising, why not hold a pen
filled with dark blood? After giving up,
one's sense of the world's pain
isn't diminished, and taste discovers
subtleties in the bitter and sweet.
Maybe there's a simpler answer:
the photographers never found them
without their miniature burning towers.
But this is a photograph of Wisława Szymborska
holding up her toxic stick with a cryptic smile.

Confession of a Retired Scholar

Though I've written seven books—
two on the practice of deconstruction
as an historical imperative, three
on philosophy and anthropology
(one of them titled *Relative Non-Relativism*),
two oft-cited works of comparative literature—
an experience has evaded
the torchbeam of erudition:

At times when I read *vers libre*
late at night; or reflect on a long-
dead writer as I brush my teeth; or
watch the wind-gashed sea and
the waves hurling snow at a cliff-face;
or absent-mindedly smooth my hair;
the image of a cherished author
—finer than a phantom—
has slipped into me.

And for a few moments—
as otherwise happens only
in love—you have caught
another's smile
in your smile.
You hold
your coffee cup
at an odd angle.

Lines in an open book
enjamb in the wrinkles
on your hand. As
you walk to the shops,
despite your stiff bones,
you possess a younger gait.

Mistranslation

I'm not sure why.
We're in the midst
of war. My friend
has remained in the tank
and thus betrayed me. I turn
the missile, aiming at the vehicle.
It explodes. I wake to screeching
trams outside the flat.
Mild morning light
gleams on the duvet's
hilly terrain.

Sparrows

Inhabiting the periphery of attention
like a mother chopping carrots in the kitchen
or a child giggling in a neighbouring room,
they lend the levity of a frond lifted on wind
as we stroll, bent to some concern.

One with the thickets and the dirty path
they hop about our feet like animate dust.
Their voices are insignificant
to the measures of politics, indifferent
as the beggar with a cardboard sign
whose life has been forgotten
except by life itself.

Is it enough that, from an aerial prospect,
hairs are numbered? With two sticks dimpling a can,
a man in the metro kneads rhythm into morning
while a river of commuters channels on.

And what about the ravaged,
whose screams are punctured by bullets
and muted by pillowed ears—multiplying
the refugees of heaven? Is it true
that serendipitous rays which lighten
a walk, an idea, a painter's strokes,
often stem from the unspent vigour
of sunflowers severed in spring?

Far from the town I halt
and notice a twig-brown body the shape of an egg,
sipping a puddle, twitching its slight
wings, where a drop lingers
a moment unbroken:
a delicate capsule
of sun.

Russian Beggar II

Ernst Barlach, 1907

The whole art of living consists in
giving up existence in order to exist.
—Goethe

Anonymous as water
  a wave of bronze:
    shawled back and head
    curling, cupped left hand and
    covered legs—the trough of the swell.

Anonymous
  you pour yourself
    into your empty hand.
      Your asking total.

But when the woman
  with rotten teeth and
    clothes rank with spirits and piss
      tugs at my sleeve in the metro,
        will I turn and stop,
          recalling this beggar
            dressed in flowing bronze?

Or are you meant
  to illustrate the Bible's words:
    I bid you put away anxious thoughts
    about food to keep you alive and
      clothes to cover your body ... Think
        of the lilies: they neither spin nor weave;
          yet I tell you, even Solomon in all his splendour
            was not attired like one of these ...?

But the beggar in Moscow
   didn't exchange her rags for these robes.
      Though he never saw her face
         did Barlach glimpse a hidden beauty
           and tailor this fabric to her soul?

Are you the muse
   of renunciation, once
      called Lady Poverty?
         The one who embraces
           those with no one and nothing,
              sustains in them the will to live,
              belief in life? The angel
                 of vagabonds and gypsies
                 sailors and prostitutes
                    the ravaged, the sick
                    the mad?

With your left hand you beg—
   the hand left out as you are left out—
      a larger empty bowl. Or
         do the ripples in your garments
            trace the contours of an ear—
               listening but distant
                  like an amphitheatre
                      between unpeopled hills?

You wait for rain like a desert valley
   (the grooves in your palm—dried-up gorges)
      wait for a shower of coins
         that will never come
         and yet you wait:

         Without desire.
         Without ambition.
         Without anxiety.
         Devoid of vanity.
         Wholly present.

Do you hear a whisper
   from the heart of things—
      the echo of the primal words
         that out of nothing
            let them be?
               Unconditioned, free
                  do you reply
                     with a singular
                        yes?

Her right hand was placed
   palm down on a patch of gritty path
      scuffed by marching soles,
         while this patch is removed
            from the huddled row of beggars,
            clean and lustrous
               it rests on a white pedestal.

Or is it a floating wooden raft
   on which you endure
      the empty sky?

THREE

Metamorphosis

Metamorphosis

I've woken from deep sleep and forgotten who I was, am. All I recall is an atmosphere of green, darkness, then incandescence. My mouth is strange—long and delicate as a pistil. My legs are spindly—comical stilts made from dried stems. Reaching out from my head, twin filaments sense vibrations, and far above my lean body extend four immense flat things. A man is admiring them, says they're more beautiful than the rose window in Chartres, compares them to an emperor's fan from the 16th century displayed in the museum of Taipei. A girl beside him says they match one of the blossoms pressed in her book. I don't know what they mean or what to do with these things.

Respite

The children now in the care of school,
she walks to the beach with a book and towel.

Reclining, her body
blends with the tan sandstone
like a natural relief. A gull
lures her eyes into the distance;
closing them, her thoughts flap upwards and
melt into the light.

A caryatid, sedimented here and there with fine
wrinkles, she stands beneath a honeycomb roof
moulded by winds, watching a shrill flock of terns
circle and dive near a row of fishermen.

Waves spread their milky foam,
hissing over a platform.
In the shadow of a boulder
a shoal of fingerlings
moves, a quickly
morphing cloud.

She gazes into the large
emerald pool.

Descending the steel ladder,
the cool embrace sings
against her skin.

Breaststroking, arms and legs
delight in the water's pressure
and give. With each kick
her feet almost dart
off on their own. Sending
thin ripples across the amnion,
she keeps her head perched,
exposed to the expanse of sky—
the blue dome sketched
with fish skeletons—while limbs
trace a primal ancestry.

Dawn

After a difficult night
the alarm wakes him
early. He lifts himself
from the bed but not entirely
from sleep—his brain,
a half-formed crystal
still precipitating out of
the solution of dreams.

Hurriedly he dresses
makes his morning coffee
departs—only glimpsing
the generous spread of light
over rooftops, foliage, roads;
the transmutation of a neighbour's
window. Yet

he feels the sun rise
on the horizon of his mind—
a pristine fountain
just beyond the city,
which trickles through
the undergrowth and
concrete channels
of his day.

Banksia Spikes

A night person, I did my best work
between 10 p.m. and 2 a.m., my mind
a black wick, aflame. When I couldn't write
I'd wander the streets. Night's adumbrations
made space for mystery. In house windows,
dark canvasses, I'd picture sleeping souls
rising through Dante's spheres. At an unlit corner
close my eyes, believe I felt the influence
like falling snow, of planets and stars.

But now when a clean winter light
bleaches the paperbark outside my window,
spreads its transparent sheet across the park
(a substitute for snow); when the glow
of a late summer afternoon fills gaps in foliage
with gold tesserae; or clouds part a little at midday
like sheep gathered around a pond; a crystal
embedded in my chest longs to refract: drawn
from my apartment I walk down the street
beside the turquoise scrolls of the sea
torn white.

Otherwise I sit at my piano, choose a score
in a major key and replay chords that harmonise
with the tone and timbre of light.

Perhaps I'm now old enough
to know the worst nightmares
are realities. Or was this conversion
written in my blood? Each day
my grandfather rode an exercise bike
out on the balcony, swam a kilometre
in the sea. But he knew darkness
far better than me.

Whatever the cause, I find myself
reiterating a religion of light,
which doesn't matter, I think,
as poetry's a kind of ritual and
I'm in good and ancient company:
Shamash, Sol, Ahura Mazda
Ra, Apollo, the Son and Sun ...
Is it really possible
to have too much light?

Returning from a walk at dusk,
I notice a banksia's countless spikes,
tall beeswax candles it bears into the night.

On the beauty of eye wrinkles

Incrementally impressed
by smiling, thinking and looking hard—
fossils in skin—presaging a far-off unity
of wisdom and joy—like shafts through clouds
they ray out from twin suns.

Glance

as the waitress takes my empty cup
we surprise each other
face
to
face
an icon on a chapel wall
glimpsed in a candle's
flicker

Double Vision

At a café in Newtown
you meet your wife and a friend—
sitting across from you on higher stools
they're Isis and Osiris
and your soul's to be weighed
against a feather.

Places you visit for the first time
yet the air seems thick, a cloak
wrapped around you by an old friend
eager to show you
what's remained and changed.

Though seldom in a church,
you sense the same liturgy
is happening elsewhere,
the spectacle a speculum
or the single image
of twin worlds.

Above a windowsill
petals seem to twirl,
dervishes whirling
with the galaxies.

A poetry evening
on the island of Samothrace.
You, speaking from the centre;
a small audience seated in an arc—
indistinct faces on the shore of night.
You recollect how during intitiation rites
the neophyte encircled by hierophants
was welcomed into the divine company.

Though you're unable to explain
these double visions, in the long interims
the world feels confined.

The Novice

Are you content with the luminous fragments
and the art of displaying them
in polished vitrines, transparent words?
The swirl of Athena's himation
in the wind's passage through an olive grove?
The face of Christ in a Byzantine mosaic—
the arc of his cheeks and eyebrows
tracing the orbit of planets, his countenance
looking down from a starry cupola?
The Gothic cathedral in Toledo
you wandered through in astonishment—
a pristine forest of the human heart,
a giant forest of prayer (it seemed as though
your blood were drawn up through the trunks,
the vaulting branches, purified) that blossoms
in the rose window? Walking by a stream at dusk
that secretly washed your soul—leaving the woods
your thoughts were clear? Birds congregating
under eucalypt-arches—warbling, squawking
laughing—the day's final chorus?
The potency that seemed to dwell
in afternoon sun on a rock face—
called to climb the mountain
you remembered Hölderlin's lines
about the god taking joy in light's play.
The feeling as you wrote one evening
the trees drew near and listened,
and later that night the sense
an angel approved, standing behind you
as in Rembrandt's portrait of Matthew?

Collapsed in defeat, how
in the embrace of a friend you felt
the support of an invisible order,
that the abyss is finite? Those mythic dreams
and conversations with the imagined dead?
Times in contemplation when your brain
seemed a husk and thoughts a thriving vine ...?
Luminous fragments, crumbs
from the gods. When
have you encountered one
mind in mind?

Scene in Music
On listening to Arvo Pärt

Bell tones fade ... A pilgrim
wanders a silent lane; his pace, largo.
Mist strays over the roofs, revealing
and concealing the moist stonework
with its sleight of hand. The arched
doors of shops are shut and locked.
A gothic cathedral stands at a corner
in another age. Halfway up the spire dissolves. Beside the entrance a raven alights
on the head of John the Evangelist, ruffles
its feathers, assumes a guardlike post.
Above the backdrop of hills:
a window of blue.

Labyrinth

Winter arrives
and wraps extra layers
around our souls.
Sappy pop songs give way
to the counterpoint of Bach.
Pine trees on the medium strip
stand upright in the incisive light.
Our minds, no longer stretches
of yellow sand, but marble labyrinths
through which we wander
tracing our steps.

Anonymous

What about the chestnut tree in the cemetery,
replete with foliage, erecting
countless steeples of blossoms—
each consisting of images
that capture the essence in a couple of strokes,
a dash of red or yellow on white—
and the perfect fragments
blown to the grass?
Does anyone else
come here to see them,
the displays of this artist
unknown even to herself?

Why I Write

*'Those ancients who in poetry presented
the golden age, who sang its happy state,
perhaps, in their Parnassus, dreamt this place.'*
—Dante, *The Divine Comedy,* Canto XXVIII

I don't write to modulate my griefs or
share my joys, though in a poem, as in music
feeling finds a key and home.

Nor do I write for recognition,
though a grateful reader's words
are raindrops to my soil.

While I wouldn't persist
were the end not a figure who speaks
for herself like the Venus de Milo, it isn't
the need for perfection—the fine
chiselling of consonants to hold
the volume of vowels—that draws me
to my desk each day.

Nor is it bibliophilia, though I recall
the moment in my teens when in books
I discovered the purest pleasure and
imagined nothing more estimable
than to bring them into being.

I don't write for revelation,
though poetry has opened rooms
in the mansion of world-mind
and led me closer to the hearth
than philosophy has.

Do I write for the fusion of thought and sense,
feeling and being—to tune these strings
and sound a harmony?

I don't write to foster the art
of double vision—to sense
the divinity in the morning gleam
on granite cliffs, whispers of the dead
in the fall of snow, the epiphany
in a stranger's friendly glance,
the way a gull floating on a thermal
becomes the singular word for grace.

I don't write to ease my conscience,
redress the past, though in moments
of recollection, the broken soil of pain
(as if time were a hidden gardener)
is transfigured into a bed of snowdrops,
roses of sublimation.

Nor do I write for posterity,
though I hope the printed sheets
make a bold flag of peace, carried
on feet that dance to the future's pulse.

I don't write solely
for these things
and could live, I believe,
without them,

I write for the expansion of the present
vital as breath to an empty lung,
for the garden that grows around me,
whether I'm in the city or on a mountain—
an invisible garden of fruit trees, hanging
wisteria and vines, honey bees, angophoras.

Turtles

*... we currently have too much humanness in the world:
too many things reflect humans, mirror humans ...*
—Martin Harrison

Glancing through a palm frond's arch,
you notice a bonsai mountain range
on an island in the pond—
five summits of igneous rock.

One sun-lacquered dome
detaches, treads towards
the water ... You find yourself
a place to sit beside the liquid sky,
its tundra and blue gorges.

The afternoon slows
to the tempo of his walk,
drawing you back
to childhood hours
lost in play, and further still
beyond your memory. You
sense the age of granite
in the almost glacial
advance.

In water, Aesop
doesn't apply. Waving
to the left and right
he seems to be heading
nowhere in labyrinthine
turns ...

Until his head
protrudes
and he looks at you
with dark sleepy eyes.
On the reptilian face
and long black neck
run veins of yellow lava.

You wonder
if there was a time
when the turtle's
skin was soft. Did
it gradually wrinkle
in water? Or
is he a sensitive soul
who suffered an early trauma,
grew the scaly epidermis
as bodily armour? In the design
you trace the line of vertebrae.

How did he turn
interior scaffolding
into a mobile home? So
now whenever he pleases
he's able to withdraw.

You note that if
the turtle could sing
he'd be a *basso profundo*.
No, deeper than any bass
he would chant with an order
of Tibetan monks.

Though he doesn't seem to know it
(perhaps he couldn't care less),
in tune again with the *Zeitgeist*
the turtle's a progressive:
totem of the slow revolution,
ambassador of poetry.

He submerges. The yellow
lilies rising from the surface—
radiant spectres. A poplar standing
against the violet-streaked sky
already absorbs night
into foliage. Hearing a creak
you turn around—the garden
gates closing.

Breakdown

Screaming
the train lurches to a halt,
beside a forest of conifers. Larches.
We draw down the windows,
look out. A wire's dangling.
The train, detached from the grid
we assume. Two women disembark
light up, mumbling in a language
I don't understand.
Beside the rusty tracks
dandelions, nettles, dry grass,
a couple of white twirling butterflies.
A breeze moves the needle-brushes
in quick cross-hatch strokes
on a transparency. Sunlight
glistens in the canopy,
among green shadows
lays straw mats on the floor.
My eyes wander slowly
like an old Labrador, settling
just there.

In Wait

We know that if the great poem comes
it will come like an eagle riding a gale
while the gulls, sparrows, finches
hide in what shelter they can find.
And we'll have to be looking
out the window across the ocean
right at that moment, and we'll need
a pen and paper to hand, and have
to exert ourselves in a protracted
sprint of composing, devote ourselves
beyond the athlete's exertion
concentrated on the body. And
the eagle's eye will glare through us
as he soars past, his shape disappear
behind a hill's tumult, and we'll
sit up through the night
trying to capture every detail, trying
to hold his full presence in mind,
and all the skills and devices
we bring to the task might prove
inadequate. For days, perhaps years,
we'll return to the manuscript
held in a desk's top drawer.
This thought comes to light—
it's been lingering in my shadow
for some time—as I sit at the end
of a jetty on a quiet lake, put
down a book, and a few ducks
approach, expecting crumbs.

Stones

for Ellen Hinsey

*'My whole surface is turned toward you,
all my insides turned away.'*
—Wisława Szymborska, 'Conversation with a Stone'

*The pebble
is a perfect creature*
—Zbigniew Herbert, 'Pebble'

We generally assume
they've no interior or soul.
When we break them open
they present a new exterior.

They're a fraction more
than nothing: a quality
of hardness, a resistance
to our touch. To our sight

bounded shapes: unmoving
inanimate. We speak of their faces
only metaphorically: lacking eyes
and mouth, at most they're blank.

But sitting by this stream
I'm struck by your simple
presence. Meeting you
the water slows and wrinkles,

rushes on. Not going anywhere
to you it's all the same whether
you're clothed in moss or bare,
dappled, in sun or shade.

The stone is worldless, Heidegger wrote.
But is this a deficiency? I agree
their detachment's perfect;
they seem outside relation—

to call them *you* a conceit—
indifferent to our distinctions:
geologic, metamorphic, igneous
sedimentary, sandstone, true or false.

But this afternoon as I worried
about what to write and do, they
and not the versatile stream,
appeared as sage—in the world

beyond the world, as though
they were primeval Buddhas
who attained complete humility
and sunken in meditation

hardly noticed death—
only an increase in light.

Val di Noto, Sicily

Excluding music,
I've never admired the Baroque—
embellishments to the point
of distraction, stucco ceilings—
but in these towns the style
reveals its naturalness: ochre-tinged façades
from the finest limestone of the gorges;
curved pediments accentuate the rhythm of hills;
composite capitals simplify
the profusion of endemic vegetation;
the Cathedral of San Giorgio crowns
the town of Modica with a flowering spike.

After a day of drizzle in Ragusa
a rainbow lends its flourish,
arches the valley. Townsfolk
who subsist with difficulty (as though
remembering the rubble of 1693) leave
their dwellings, amble the rich streets
before the evening meal.

Late sunlight restores a wide piazza
where neighbours sit on benches and talk—
wearing the surroundings like a laurel wreath
that belongs to all and to no one.

Moon over the Sea

A dark grey expanse
a lucent strip of blue
a long bank of cloud
silent and absorbing
as a Rothko.

At the centre, the tilted
round candle of the moon
whose beeswax melts
in a trail across the shaky
sea-table.

You sit on a bench,
and looking more deeply
see that it's a wafer
transmuted by the sun;
invisible hands lift it
before the iconostasis.

Though alchemists identified
the moon with silver and
in an hour they'll be right again,
now on the dark floor
flickers a gold mosaic.

In the deep blue cupola
constellations crystallise—
the prototype of a church
you chanced on years ago
in a backstreet of Rome,
save the Southern Cross
and Emu in the Sky.

Tracing the arc of the ecliptic
you notice the row of giant pines
standing along the park's border,
austere angels.

View from the Shore
Sicily

Over the darkening water
the distant mountains are simplified
to magenta silhouettes—erasing all trace
of apartment blocks constructed in the sixties and
the growling motorway that tunnels through the limestone;
they're almost immaterial, a watercolour landscape.

Behind them is a realm of light,
enigmatic as portrayals of a golden age
in the distant past or future, outside time.
An arc of clouds hovers around the illumined air—
a mosaic of six-winged seraphs with feathers of flame
guarding a cathedral entrance. Only our eyes
cross into that realm. Over small waves
that turn and break their darkened glass
on the shore, a gull departs.

Notes

'Translation'
The image of a phonograph at the end of this poem bears a connection to Rilke's imaginative thought experiment in 'Primal Sound' ('Ur-Geräusch'). A translation of this text can be found in Rainer Maria Rilke, *Where Silence Reigns*, trans. G. Craig Houston (New York: New Directions, 1978), pp. 51–56.

'Horizon of Alps (K)'
The 'k' in the title and at the end of this poem should be pronounced like the 'c' in 'cat' but without any vowel sound succeeding it.

'Annunciation'
This poem should be read from left to right across the page (the columns are not independent).

'Petrifaction'
This poem was sparked by the sculpture *Hilje* by Clara Hali, which was exhibited in the 2014 Sculpture by the Sea, Bondi-Tamarama.

'The Field and Tonic'
This poem should be read starting from the bottom (the title) and upwards from the left, then across to the right and down.

'Russian Beggar II'
Ernst Barlach's sculpture *Russian Beggar II* is exhibited in Ernst Barlach Haus, Hamburg, Germany. The epigraph is taken from Goethe's *Maxims and Reflections* (translated by Thomas Bailey Saunders). The quotation from the Bible in this poem is taken from Luke 12.22-4 in *The New English Bible* (Oxford: Oxford University Press, 1970), p. 91.

'The Novice'
The mention of Hölderlin alludes to the opening lines of the second section of Friedrich Hölderlin's poem 'Heimkunft' ('Homecoming').

'Why I Write'
The epigraph is taken from Allen Mandelbaum's translation of Dante's *The Divine Comedy* (New York: Alfred A. Knopf, 1995), p. 350. The conception of this poem is in part indebted to Vicente Aleixandre's poem 'Para quién escribo' ('Who I Write For').

'Turtles'
The epigraph is taken from 'Postscript: Connecting: a dialogue between Deborah Bird Rose and Martin Harrison', *TEXT* Special Issue 20: Writing Creates Ecology and Ecology Creates Writing, eds. Martin Harrison, Deborah Bird Rose, Lorraine Shannon and Kim Satchell, October 2013, p. 2.

'Stones'
The first epigraph is taken from Wisława Szymborska, 'Conversation with a Stone', in *View with a Grain of Sand: Selected Poems*, trans. Stanisław Barańczak and Clare Cavanagh (London: Faber and Faber, 1996), p. 31. The second epigraph is taken from Zbigniew Herbert, 'Pebble', in *Selected Poems*, trans. Peter Dale Scott and Czesław Miłosz (Harmondsworth: Penguin, 1968), p. 108. Lines 3–4 of the poem allude to and paraphrase notions found in Martin Heidegger's philosophy and Szymborska's above-mentioned poem. In his essay 'The Origin of the Work of Art' (1935/36) Heidegger elaborates that the stone's heaviness denies penetration: 'If we attempt such a penetration by breaking open the rock, it still does not display in its fragments anything inward that has been opened up.' Heidegger proceeds to describe 'the earth' more generally as 'that which shrinks from every disclosure and constantly keeps itself closed up' (Heidegger, *Basic Writings*, ed. David Farrell Krell [London: Routledge, 1993], p. 172). These formulations are strikingly similar to Szymborska's lines, in which the voice of the stone states: 'Even if you break me to pieces, / we'll all still be closed. You can grind us to sand, / we still won't let you in' (p. 30). Heidegger makes and discusses the claim that 'the stone is worldless' (quoted in the poem) in *The Fundamental Concepts of Metaphysics* (*Die Grundbegriffe der Metaphysik*).

www.ingramcontent.com/pod-product-compliance
Lightning Source LLC
Chambersburg PA
CBHW020336170426
43200CB00006B/402